Useful for Business

The Work Hacks of Great Japanese Men

What would you do ?

Preface

I've always liked history, and so I have read numerous amounts of books about it throughout my life. After I grew up and became independent, history felt more close to me than ever. I think it's because I've had more situations where I could think, what historical figures must have thought and done, if they were in my situation. It was Bismarck who said, "Wise men learn from history, while fools learn from experience". And thankfully, the history of Japan is filled with amazing figures who we could learn so much from.

It will be my pleasure, if the slice of history I present to you in this book will be useful to you as a case by case study.

Table of Contents

Chapter 3 Work Hacks from the Edo ~ Meiji Period

Chapter 1
Work Hacks of Ancient Japanese Gods

Okuninushi "Master of the Great Land" – Making Use of the People Around You

Okuninushi, the founder of Japan. Worshiped at the Izumo Taisha

Okuninushi was a name later given by Susanoo.

Being the 7th descendant of Susanoo, he was originally

named Oonamuchi, while Okuninushi means "Master of the Great Land".

Being the god that founded Japan, and later gifting the country to Amatsukami, if Susanoo is the superstar of Japanese myth Okuninushi is surely the Japanese hero.

When we say a "Japanese hero", what we mean is that even though he was weak at first, he became strong through his own effort and the help of others. Just like Kenshiro, the anime captain from the "Hokuto no Ken" series.

Although he was one of the first to be bullied in the entire history of Japan, he was able to achieve such an accomplishment of creating a whole country.

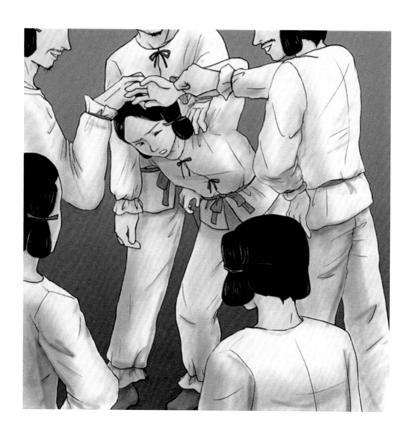

And there are a lot of things we can learn from that.

The story of Ookuninushi starts from the story called "Inaba-no-Shiro-Usagi (the white rabbit of Inaba)", found in the "Kojiki".

The young Okuninushi had many brothers (more than 80), who constantly bullied Okuninushi.

One day, the brothers set out to win the heart of Yagami-hime, famous for being incredibly beautiful. Okuninushi also set out with them, but he was essentially just an errand boy, carrying their luggage.

The brothers who went ahead with free hands stumble upon a rabbit who was red because its skin had been peeled off.

Looking at the suffering rabbit, the brothers lie saying that seawater would heal the wound.

Believing the brothers the rabbit bathes itself in seawater, but obviously it stings and the rabbit suffers even more.

Finally catching up, Okuninushi asks the rabbit what had happened. The rabbit tells him he had come from the Island of Oki, and how he had tricked a shark into taking him oversea.

Okuninushi, without scolding the rabbit, tells the rabbit to bathe itself in the river and to use pollen to heal its wounds. The rabbit did as he was told, and the pain went away.

In a sense, the rabbit got it deserved, since he tricked a shark in the first place. However, instead of condemning the rabbit, Okuninushi sympathizes towards him, understanding that he has already gone through enough.

The rabbit says to Okuninushi, "Those gods would never be able to take the hand of Yagami-hime. You are the one who deserves her."

And, low and behold, when the brothers and Okuninushi arrive at Yagami-hime's place, the princess ignores the brothers and chooses Okuninushi.

The enraged brothers, angry that the princess chose the weak errand boy, decide to kill Okuninushi.

They first call Okuninushi to help hunt a boar, saying "we'll send the boar your way, so catch it at the foot of the mountain!" Okuninushi waits at the foot of the mountain, but instead of a boar, a giant stone roaring with fire comes crashing down on him. Okuninushi was burned to death.

His mother, in her sadness asks Amatsukami to send Akagai hime and Hamaguri hime to heal her son. The two goddesses come, and Akagai hime collects the body parts from the rocks and Hamaguri hime uses her milk to rise Okuninushi from the dead.

Learning that Okuninushi had been risen from the dead, the brothers, in their fear, decide to murder him again.

They cut down a big tree to create a trap, and tricked
Okuninushi into his death.

The mother asks Amatsukami for help and successfully saves Okuninushi again. However scared that her son might be murdered again she takes him to the country of Susanoo.

Even the brothers cannot hurt Okuninushi if Susanoo is the one protecting him.

At Susanoo's country, Okuninushi meets princess Suseri, the daughter of Susanoo, and instantly falls in love.

Susanoo gives Okuninushi numbers of challenges, but with the help of Suseri Okununushi manages to overcome them all.

In the end, the lovers run away while Susanoo is asleep. Susanoo finds out and chases them, but gives up saying "Use your weapon to defeat your brothers. After that is over, you shall rule Japan". Okuninushi was no longer weak.

The brothers were no match for the now powerful Okuninushi.

With the brothers gone, Okuninushi starts the process of building the country. As he contemplates how to actually accomplish it, Sukunahiko, (said to be the origin of the Japanese story Inch Boy) arrives to his aid as an advisor.

However after a while, the country went back into what it

originally was. As he was contemplating what he can do, Okuninushi sees a ball of light approaching him over the sea. When Okuninushi asks it, "Who are you?" it replied,

"I am your spirit, both good and bad. Worship me on this land and you can create your country, don't worship me and it would be impossible." Okuninushi did as he was told.

Maybe the ball of light was his own voice telling him to proceed with confidence.

That being said, this ball of light has been worshiped as "Omononushi" at the Omiwa shrine in Nara, and since it worships a god this shrine is said to be the oldest shrine in history.

What we can learn from Okuninushi's way of working is,

Listening to Others
Be nice to the people around you so that you always have people on your side
Work with others, not by yourself

Rather than stubbornly trying to do it all by yourself, admit the things you can't do or don't know how, and ask for help. The bullied and weak Okuninushi went on to create a whole country.

The kindness, respect and open heart that was behind this bullied boy was his strength, and this is the way we all should be.

In the end he hands over the country he made to Amatsukami.

He left this decision to his son and heir Kotoshironushi, but it must have been hard to give up a country.

This is only speculation, but in the ancient writing two ways of governing come up, "Ushihaku" and "Shirasu".

Ushihaku is the way of becoming the owner of a country, ruling over the people and land as the king reigning over them all. It's safe to say almost all monarchy follow this style.

On the other hand, Shirasu is for the people to assemble in a sort of meeting in front of the authoritative figure (In this case Amatsukami) exchanging information and ruling over the land through discussion.

Even in the case of transferring the country, thee two systems are compared through Okuninushi, with him concluding that although he has used the Ushihaku way, Shirasu was better.

Thanks to his decision (In reality said to be done by his son), the system of Shirasu was used throughout Japanese history.

Even Amatsukami respected Okuninushi's decision highly, constructing a temple to show it. It has been found that this temple was a wooden structure of over 48 meters, one of the largest wooden structures throughout history.

When the Emperor and Empress of Japan visited Izumo shrine in 2003, he read this poem;

国譲り

祀られましし

大神の

奇しき御業を

偲びて止まず

<Translation>

Giving away a country

I cannot stop respecting the amazing act of the great god worshipped here

Constructing a country and giving it away. This was Okuninushi's accomplishment.

Even though he was weak, a coward and was bullied, by being kind to the people around him and using their strengths, he managed to achieve such a great accomplishment. This is what we can learn from the way Okuninushi lived his life.

＊Try applying Okuninushi's life to yours

Even when bullied, rather than sulking he showed kindness to those in need, and eventually founded a country.

<Questions>

Who is someone you want to be kind to, even though they are not necessarily strong?

Okuninushi became strong by overcoming the challenges given by Susanoo. What do you need in order to elevate your ability?

Okuninushi respected the opinions of the wise and small god, Sukunahiko. Do you listen to the opinions of others?

Japan's god of wisdom, Omoikane

Omoikanemikoto is worshipped in the Togakushi shrine in Ichihara, Nagano, and also at the Kishyo shrine in Tokyo.

The kanji for Omoikane are "思金神 "or "思兼神", and sometimes even "八意思金神".

These kanji's represents Omoikene as the ideal image of human intelligence. In the ancient Japanese writing of

"Kojikiden", it is written that he has the knowledge of numerous people all in one soul.

Omoikane means to gather large amounts of wisdom in to one.

He is part of this chapter, because like the present, the history of gods is also a one about solving many problems.

How did they deal with their problems?

The answer is pretty clear when you consider the fact that Omoikane is the god of wisdom.

Omoikane comes up a lot in Japanese mythology, but probably one of his most famous story is giving the wisdom to bring out Amaterasu Omikami from his hiding.

Amaterasu coming out from the cave.

A little before the story, Amaterasu and Susanoo had a conflict, in which Susanoo won and proceeded to commit acts of violence. Dismayed, Amaterasu withdrew into a cave. Without Amaterasu, the god of sun, the world went into darkness. To fix this, eight million gods came together to discuss, and concluded they should ask Omoikane for help. Omoikane suggests a clever plan.

He said, first let's celebrate!

Opening the stone door blocking the cave from the outside is difficult, so he decided to try opening it from Amaterasu's side. Clever. Not from the outside, but from the inside. The gods decided to focus on this point.

Not only that, they placed Tajikarao right next to the stone door that when Amaterasu opens the door, he can throw it away so that no one could use it anymore. They prepared the plan so that Amaterasu won't go back in to the cave again after they brought him out. With the preparations set, they started the festival.

They first brought a rare bird from a foreign country, and made it cry to make Amaterasu curious.

The blacksmith god, Ishikoridomoe made a mirror, and the Tamatsu god Tamanooyanomikoto creates a sphere gem, and the two combine it using cotton to create a Tamagushi. And by having a festival, the plan was to make Amaterasu wonder, why everyone was having a good time without him.

As the god of words, Amanokoyane swung the Tamaki and sang, Amenouzume lightened up the party by performing a strip show.

When Amaterasu, curiously peeks out of the cave, Amanouzume explains,

"We are celebrating because a god more important than you

has arrived"

With this, Amaterasu gets more and more curious about what is going on. He opens the door, and to his surprise sees himself in a mirror placed outside. Seizing the opportunity, Tajikaro drags Amaterasu out of the cave, throws away the stone door, and the gods succeeded in bringing Amaterasu back to the outside world. The stone door that Tajikaro threw flew all the way to Togakushi shirn, where it is still worshiped.

The moral of the story

Rather than forcefully dragging something out,
Make them come out themselves.

Always be prepared to seize the opportunity.

Omoikane brought back light to the world by hosting a festival.

In other cases,
Participated in the transferring of the country

Amatsukami (god in heaven) ordered Okuninushi who ruled the country on the ground to give up the country to him. Amatsukami sent multiple messengers to figure out the process, but things don't work out. In the end, they sent

Takenomikaduchi, the god of war to forcefully get the country.

In this particular case, even Omoikane made 2 mistakes in selecting the appropriate person for the job, and only succeeded on his third try.

This could mean that choosing the right person for the job is difficult even for a god.

And from the fact that they used the god of war, we can see that they were running out of options.

The Decent

Omoikane played a part when Amaterasu's grandson, Ninigi descended down to Japan.

Ninigi had just received Japan as the heir of Amaterasu, and had been assigned the job to rule over it.

Omoikane came down with him to help govern the land. After that, he went to the country of Shinano, and created Chichibu.

Omoikane, the god of wisdom, always showed his skill in times of change and difficulty, but even he made mistakes, as shown in the transferring of the country. What we should take from all this, is that even the smartest beings makes mistakes.

＊Try applying Omoikane's wisdom to yourself

Omoikane was the god with the wisdom to solve even the most complicated enigmas. He has provided the solution to bring Amaterasu out of hiding, and faced numerous, troublesome tasks.

<Questions>

You want customers to purchase your product or services, but customers don't. How could you make customers interested in the product and services so that they'll come to you?

The transferring of the country was a big checkpoint in Japanese mythology. It is the business equivalent of personnel renewal, and succession. What would be the most successful placement of personnel?

Chapter 2
Work Hacks of Sengoku Warlords

Takeda Shingen – The Most Powerful Tactic Starts with the Confidence to Win

Takeda Shingen led the Takeda Cavalry, the most powerful cavalry during the Sengoku Period

Takeda Shingen (1521 ~1573) was known not only for his talent in war, but for his ability as a ruler.

Although the Takeda family ruled the land of Kai, Kai did not unify until Takeda Shingen's father, Nobutora brought peace to the land after years of conflict. With peace, the Takeda family also obtained power. Nobutora goes on to show his skill of diplomacy and further strengthens his power by signing treaties with strong allies. Nobutora was the one who created the foundations of Kai.

Nobutora, disliking the intelligent Shingen attempts to set Shingen's brother, Nobushige as the next ruler of the land. It was quite normal for families to fight within each other during the Sengoku Period.

The Decision to banish his father

When Shingen turned 21, he banished Nobutora, his own father. Around this time, Nobutora had become tyrannical, and his own people and subordinates were starting to turn on him. So when Shingen asked his brother Nobushige if he would follow Shingen or their father, Nobushige replied by saying "I will follow you, big brother". When Shingen said, "to follow me is to work under me, are you alright with that?" Nobushige replied "Yes".

When Nobutora's closest associates started to ally with Shingen, he finally had enough power to banish his father.

He asked the Imagawa family to take care of his father, sending them nearly one hundred million yen each year.

Shingen took over the land not for himself, but for the whole family, which was something his subordinates understood well, including his brother.

After his father was banished, Shingen proceeded to install systems to better listen to the voices of his associates.

He understood that people will listen to your opinion better if they had already said their opinions, so he always listened to the voices of his people and made decisions in a way that his men agreed. Because his country was in the mountains, the only way to gain more strength was to expand his dominion, so he sent his forces to Shinano, the adjacent country to his. Shingen also constantly rewarded warlords who did well.

However, constant war only brings discontent of the people. Expansion is necessary, but constant war is not possible.

The solution Shingen reached was to "fight wars without losing, and fight without being damaged".

Especially when invading other countries, Shingen planned every moved, utilized spies, obtained as much information as possible and attempted to turn his enemy into an ally many times.

On the other hand, all out wars were rare. Even at the famous fight of Kawanaka Island, a large scale battle was only done once.

He also actively searched for good assets, taking in a number of intelligent and talented subordinates regardless of their social status.

This was a fresh way in those times and Shingen often rewarded those with success.

Obtaining Information

By understanding every aspect of the enemy such as size, weapons, ability, and movement, Shingen always figured out a way to win the battle, then on top of that created a plan to win without fighting, saving war as a last resort.

Shingen only lost 3 battles in his life of over 70 years.

Know the enemy and know yourself

While learning every possible thing about the enemy, Shingen also worked hard to not let others learn about his own army. Know the enemy but don't let them know you. This was the principle that made winning even more probable.

Furinkazan

Furinkazan is the famous banner of Takeda Shingen.

Meaning, "Fast like the wind, quiet like the forest, vicious like the fire and unmovable like the mountain".

War costs money, and instead of making strong castles like others, Shingen used that money to invade others.

One of his famous quote is, "man is stone, man is castle, mercy for allies, revenge for enemy "

One aspect of this quote is surely his trust towards his men, but the other aspect is that once a man sets out to rule a land, he cannot return.

Meaning that their duty is to preserve it no matter what, to expand, to make the land rich, and as rulers of a land, they have to act like Shingen in their land.

Through this way of thinking, expansion meant rulers with the spirit of Shingen were placed throughout the country.

Through this process, the trust between Shingen and his men became even stronger.

But that wasen't Shingen's only achievement.

He accelerated the construction of rice fields, the maintenance of roads so that his armies can move faster, and he developed gold mines and created a new currency called Koushuukin.

He did not take choosing his successor lightly. He treated his first born son so strictly that he died, and even when Katsuyori, the next in line became the ruler Shingen always had doubts.

Although the Takeda army, thanks to Shingen and his men, were considered the strongest during the Sengoku period, they were extremely careful when it came to choosing their heir. In the end, Shingen named Katsuyori's son to be his heir, and Katsuyori retreated himself and supported the Takeda family through his son. Not only that, Shingen near his death said,

"Keep my death quiet for 3 years, and rely on Uesugi Kenshin in Echigo. That is the only way the Takeda family will survive"

He relied on his nemesis because even though Kenshin was an enemy, Shingen respected his skill in war and his intelligence, praising him as "Japan's greatest man" in his later years.

On the other hand Uesugi Kenshin focused on a fighting style that avoided defeat, and said himself "I cannot surpass Shingen on this point".

Katsuyori, who in reality was the virtual successor of Shingen, had skill in war and the maximum territory of the Takeda family was achieved during his era. However he constantly had doubts mostly due to his personality, and his choice to ignore Shingen's will was what eventually led to the extinction of the Takeda family.

Shingen's work hack

I am not the priority.
Listen to the opinion of subordinates.
Collect information first, then figure out a way not to lose.

Shingen's style was to advance only when he was certain he could "win".

To win the fight before the battle was how Shingen fought, and he always treated his men with care. By providing rewards for those who did well, Shingen brought out the most from his subordinates, and by trusting them to rule over small pieces of land, and communicating with them constantly, Shingen had a trusting and close relationship with his men.

These were the techniques Shingen used. A lot of these tips are useful in modern times as well.

*Try applying Shingen's lifestyle to yourself

Shingen was one of the greatest generals in history, leading the strongest cavalry during the Sengoku period. He was talented not only in war, but in ruling as well.

<Questions>

Shingen banished Nobutora, his own father so that he could sit on the throne, and always prioritized the greater good over himself. However banishing your father is not an easy decision. What is the "greater good" for your job?

Shingen spent a lot of effort bringing in talented men, letting those with skill work whatever their status was, and those who were chosen worked hard and earned rewards for their efforts. Are there people around you who might show his skill given the right opportunity?

Shingen, who was good at war always knew the importance of getting information and learning about the enemy and yourself. Are you obtaining enough information?

Shingen was great at keeping his men together, and in his later years he never built a castle. This was proof that he had a strong relationship with his men, and Shingen's idea of giving land to his subordinates and making them rulers of their land is a good one, and let to the unity of his armies. What are some ways to have a better relationship with your subordinates?

Uesugi Kenshin - Achievement is in the legs "Acting more than others brings victory"

One of the popular generals of the Sengoku Period, Uesugi Kenshin

Like Takeda Shingen, who becomes Kenshin's rival,

Kenshin has left many meaningful words.

He is definitely one of my favorite generals, but he is known to fight in a rather peculiar way.

Although he fought with Shingen a couple times at the battle of Kawanaka island, in later years Shingen calls his nemesis Kenshin, "Japan's greatest man", and before his death he tells his men to rely on Kenshin in need. Kenshin was such a remarkable man that even Shingen respected hi.

Here is one of Kenshin's quotes.

Luck is in the heavens, Armor is on the chest, and Achievement is in the legs.

What does "achievement is in the legs" mean?

Basically, act.

This quote is actually part of a much longer passage, but he writes that accomplishing achievements is what leads to rewards and promotion.

Which is pretty obvious, but to move, and to move even more is important because acting the same amount as the next guy doesn't lead to anything. Therefore, take as much action as possible.

That is what

"Achievement is in the legs"

Means. This is a valuable lesson even in the present. Doing nothing sitting at the desk doesn't lead to anything. Go outside, act. This is true for any time in history. This is a philosophy seen in Hideyoshi and Nobunaga as well. He also writes about the heart.

"The 16 laws of the heart

When the heart is not lost, it does not find fault in others
When the heart has no pride, it finds the good in man
When the heart has consideration its loyalty is great
When the heart isn't vulgar it does not desire
When the heart has courage it does not regret
When the heart is free of doubt it is peaceful
When the heart can endure it is prepared
When the heart is free of anger its words are soft
When the heart does not covet it does not fight others
When the heart has no evil thoughts, it raises others
When the heart is right it does not fear
When the heart has no deception it saves others

When the heart is selfless it does not suspect others

When the heart has no greed it is true to duty

When the heart is not selfish it does not lose love

When the heart is not clouded it is peaceful"

Kenshin is said to have been intelligent from an early age, clearly seen in his impressive writings. He passes away at the age of 49, and it is told that this is the poem he wrote before his departure;

四十九年　一睡の夢　一期の栄華　一盃の酒

(49 years, a short dream, a momentary glory, a cup of liquor)

Compared to the information filled society of today, the education of generals back in the day must have been minimal. However, Kenshin was skilled in art and poems.

These poems are beautiful even for us.

Kenshin lived through the age of war and chaos, but it seems that he always valued the truth and genuineness of things.

In the way of the warrior, luck is in the heavens, armor is on the chest and achievement is in the legs.

Even in these words, you can see his behaviorism.

Whether in battle or debate, he valued taking action.

And even though he was vicious at times,

"This body will one day be gone. However, this heart, and my ways will stay on this land for eternity, and be passed on for generations. That is because I represent the truth"

You can call that one strong confidence in yourself, but at the same time it feels like words spoken from the soul.
He was an incredible warlord.
These were the words of Uesugi Kenshin,

＊Try applying Uesugi Kenshin's way to yourself.

One of the popular generals of the Sengoku period, he was skilled not only in war, but also in ruling. He was trusted deeply due to his way of valuing the truth.

<Questions>

Uesugi Kenshin was good at war, but as his words say "Luck is in the heavens, armor is on the chest and achievements is in the legs", Kenshin believed that acting is the key to success. Are you acting enough?

Commonly called as the general of righteousness, Kenshin says that his way of righteousness is something eternal, and that it is our duty to be an example for our descendants. And he accomplished it. What is "righteousness" for you?

Oda Nobunaga - Thinking Outside the Box

Oda Nobunaga's foresight was forged by thinking outside the box

A general from the Sengoku, Azuchimomoyama period (1534 ~ 1582), he was the ruler of the small country of Owari (now Aichi prefecture). Although he was considered stupid and odd, he came close to unifying the entire country of Japan, only to commit suicide at the last step due to the betrayal of his subordinate, Akechi Mitsuhide.

One of the greatest generals of all time, what he expected from his followers was to

"Know what to do without being told, or understand quickly when told what to do"

Oda Nobunaga is said to have valued information greatly.
1. obtain information quickly
2. identify the problem from the information
3. consider the problem and form a solution/plan
4. decide the priorities within the plan

Oda Nobunaga used his information in this way, but he also was careful in the quality of information and paid close attention to reports, according to his memorandum.

The battle that made Oda Nobunaga famous was the battle of Okehazama.

With only 2000 men in his army, he faced the army of Imakawa who had 25000 men, more than 10 times of that of Nobunaga's army.

Oda Nobunaga, against all odds, claimed complete victory

by taking the head of Imakawa Yoshimoto, the enemy general.

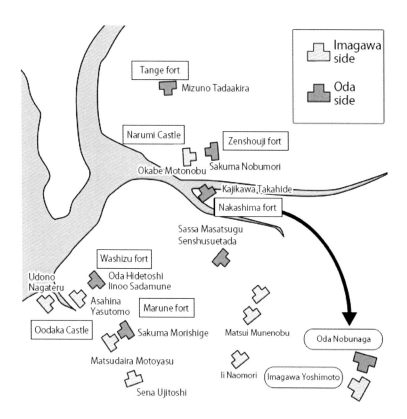

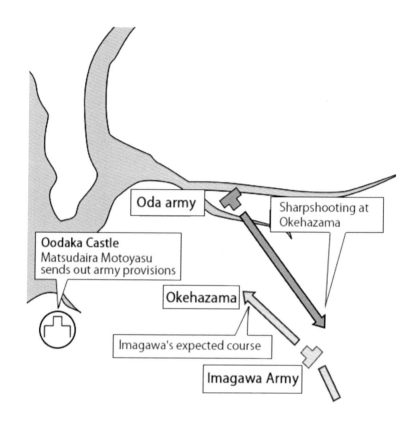

Oda army

Sharpshooting at Okehazama

Oodaka Castle
Matsudaira Motoyasu
sends out army provisions

Okehazama

Imagawa's expected course

Imagawa Army

How did Oda Nobunaga manage to win?

While many say it was due to the successful surprise attack, the true cause of victory was the ability to gain information quickly, and to analyze the situation accurately.

During the celebration of victory, Yanada Masatsuna, was rewarded the most, even though no one knew who he was.

Everyone expected that Hattori Shouheita, and Mouri Shinsuke who took the head of the enemy general Imakawa, would be given credit and be rewarded the most. Confused, Nobunaga's followers pursued him for an explanation.

He replied, "In the first place, all of you decided to die in battle when we were discussing strategies. I did not accept this. What would our families do when the head of the family dies in battle? What about the Oda family? It felt too irresponsible. I didn't have any clever ideas or knowledge, but Yanada here provided us with valuable information and a suggestion of a plan. We won the war thanks to him".

The information that Yanada provided was that

1. Numerous farmers had been sent as soldiers, and were starting to cook near Okehazama
2. Cooking was also starting in the nearby Denrakuhazama
3. The sky is looking strange

He was even more specific, saying
1. The food at Okehazama was lousy
2. The food at Denrakuhazama was luxurious

Then Yanada suggested this plan to Nobunaga.

From the information, we can conclude that the normal foot soldiers are eating at Okehazama, while the generals and the high class warriors are eating at Denrakuhazama.

"From this, and the fact that we can assume there would be a storm at tomorrow noon due to the strange sky, we should attack Denrakuhazama with the storm and focus on killing the enemy generals first.

They won by executing this plan.

Without Yanada's information and a plan, they would have definitely not been able to win the war. And that is why Yanada was rewarded the most.

Nobunaga said "I want you to be someone who knows what to do without being told, or quickly understand when told what to do. Don't be someone who doesn't understand even when told".

Meaning, we should predict the near future from the information we gather, and figure out the most successful way to deal with the problem.

Nobunaga had been called an "Utsuke (meaning a retard)" from a very young age, but he had learned a lot by walking around the city and talking to merchants, entertainers, monks and farmers.

He probably understood the power of information from a very early age.

Even after this, Nobunaga goes on to fight many battles, but each time he gathers information quickly, and comes up with clever tactics to lead his army to victory. You can see how much he values information from the fact that he rewards the provider of information the most.

It was rare for a general to value information as much as Nobunaga in his time.

He naturally learned how to value information and to break the common sense of his time, but his real strength was the ability to think outside the box. Thanks to this, he was later on able to organize gun troops, come up with military separation, and this may have even lead to the famous burning of Hiei Mountain.

Either way, through his use of intelligence he went from the ruler of a small country to near conquer of a nation. His way with information and his ability to think outside the box are both things we can use in modern times.

＊Try applying Oda Nobunaga's way and knowledge to yourself

Nobunaga is without doubt a special existence in Japanese history, with the astounding ability of both acting strategically and creating new ideas.

<Questions>

At the battle of Okehazama, strategically attacked the heart of the army, and won. The main cause of victory was of course, his utilization of intelligence. Do you have enough information? What are your sources?

Nobunaga's symbol and also his will, "Tenkafubu (bring peace and prosperity to the nation), was chosen after he had conquered Gifu, the country next to his. What is your will that you show to others?

To accomplish his goals, he used General Ashikaga's charisma. What are some brands you can use for your benefit?

In the battle against the Takeda cavalry, Nobunaga used the most advanced weapon, guns. He aligned his gun troops in 3 lines so that they could rapidly fire towards the enemy, and ended up defeating the strongest army at the time. He claimed victory by using advanced technology with an innovative idea. How can you use new technology in innovative ways?

Toyotomi Hideyoshi - the Economical Mind that impressed Oda Nobunaga

Toyotomi Hideyoshi, the farmer who unified an entire nation was outstanding in work and foresight

Toyotomi Hideyoshi (1537 ~ 1598)

Starting out as a farmer in the country of Owari, he started to wander around selling needles from the age of 15, and ended up working for Oda Nobunaga.

Some say he was originally a merchant, or that he was born in a mountain tribe, but the truth is unknown. What is known is that he heard the rumors of Oda Nobunaga (particularly how he promotes and rewards those skill, whatever their status was), and went to work for him. From them, as it is written in his autobiography, he "worked until his bones wore out". Hideyoshi gave his full effort towards every work that was given to him, and slowly he rose to power.

The story of how Hideyoshi warmed Nobunaga's sandals with his body on a cold winter day is famous. Of course, Nobunaga first thought Hideyoshi had been sitting on his sandals and scolded him, but when he learned the truth, he was very pleased.

Toyotomi Hideyoshi's foresight began by choosing his boss

Due to the old customs of the time, it was difficult to rise to power even if you had skill and potential. However, the rumor of Oda Nobunaga and his ways of breaking the custom had been famous. Oda Nobunaga was as strict as he was open minded.

It's safe to say that Hideyoshi bet his career on Nobunaga.

To be approved by Nobunaga was a great motive for Hideyoshi.

He was first appreciated when Hideyoshi cut the cost needed for firewood.

When Nobunaga asked his followers, why the cost of firewood was increasing, they replied "We're doing as we always have". Hideyoshi raised his hand to solve this problem.

Hideyoshi told Nobunaga," Sir, I will fix the cost of firewood", and he was given the job.

Hideyoshi first went to the site and considered these things.

1. The route of which firewood comes to the castle (particularly the efficiency of it)
2. If the amount of firewood that is bought is appropriate

He decided to focus on these two points.

First, for the route of firewood, he found out that various routes existed.

He also found out the one of these routes had been a major source of loss.

Hideyoshi cursed the guy that did nothing about the route, but proceeded to consider the amount of firewood.

So, he thoroughly searched for any waste of firewood.

From the kitchen to heat, to even baths, Hideyoshi researched the number of firewood used in each place.

He concluded that there were many possible solutions in both the amount and use of firewood, and was shocked that his predecessor had done no work at all.

There were numbers of bribery going on in the trade as well, but pursuing those were not important, since the importance was to make the amount and use of firewood appropriate.

Even more, changing the trade route without proper consideration may result to increase in crime.

So Hideyoshi thought.

For the route, changing the routes one by one have many problems.

He decide it would be better to get rid of the brokers all together.

This was his conclusion.

And as he walked around the villages, he realized that there were many dead trees, and asked the head of the villages if he could have them. Even more he offered to either reduce taxes, or give them saplings. He went around the villages offering the two choices.

What Hideyoshi did was

1. Created an industry of trees (successfully got rid of brokers)
2. Managed to get firewood for free
3. In return, offered tax reduction or saplings

As a result

1. Firewood became free
2. Tax reduction led to a decrease in income
3. Saplings became an expense

However, thanks to Hideyoshi the cost of firewood went down to 10% of its original cost.

Even more, thanks to the saplings the environment got better.

Nobunaga, hearing these accomplishments, was pleased saying "The monkey can do his job".

Hideyoshi was good at these types of work, and with his skill approved he began to surpass others.

Here's another story.

Nobunaga's main castle was Kiyosu castle, but one year it was hit by a terrible storm.

100 men were assigned to fix the castle but work was slow, and the manager only yelled at his workers.

Seeing this, Nobunaga fired the manager and assigned Hideyoshi instead.

Hideyoshi first researched the damaged parts thoroughly, and divided the entire castle in to 10 parts.

He told the workers,

"Divide yourselves in to 10 groups! Choose who to group up with amongst yourselves. I don't know which one of you are friends and which are enemies. I doubt its fun working with someone you hate. It's stressful as well. Now, hurry up and pick your leaders. "

And on top of that he said,

"The lord will handsomely reward the group that finishes their work first"

By saying this, he made them compete, and finished the repair in a blink of an eye.

Hideyoshi always understood how people operated, and he used his talent throughout his life in governing, war, diplomacy and even in creating a nation.

His boss, Nobunaga was known for being a rationalist, but Hideyoshi was even more so, and in any circumstance Hideyoshi would assess the situation and problem, and formulated a solution. Since Hideyoshi was capable of this way of thinking, he got along with Nobunaga.

In his years of promotion, there must have been some jealousy and attack from his colleagues. But, Hideyoshi, with his positive personality, and his thoughtfulness was able to overcome these challenges without breaking a sweat, and later on succeeded in unifying Japan. Hideyoshi's work style is shone in his words spoken in later years; "I worked until my bones wore out". He worked hard, and thought hard.

* Try Applying Hideyoshi's workstyle to yours.

Toyotomi HIdeyoshi's promotion is rare even in world history. From farmer to lord of Japan, his workstyle is something to learn from.

<Questions.>

When ordered to reduce the cost of firewood from Nobunaga, Hideyoshi first researched the purchase route and amount of firewood and checked its efficiency, and formed a solution by checking each use of firewood and making sure the appropriate amount was used. Is the way you spend your budget efficient? Is the price of your products appropriate?

When repairing a damaged castle, Hideyoshi divided the area into 10 parts, assigned a group to each part and made them compete using a reward system, and successfully repaired the castle quickly. Is there a way to make your work into a team based game?

Tokugawa Ieyasu - Burden makes man

This is portrait of him right after his massive defeat against Takeda Shingen at the battle of Mikatagahara.

He wanted to know what kind of expression he had on his face after his defeat.

After this battle, he kept this portrait right next to him all through his life.

It was a message to himself to never make the same mistake twice, mistakes that were made through his fear and arrogance.

Although Ieyasu was defeated completely, it is said he respected Shingen throughout his life.

While Ieyasu's plan was completely seen through by Shingen in Ieyasu's early years, in his later years you can see Ieyasu's admiration through the fact he invited many of Takeda's men to come under his protection after the Takeda family had collapsed.

Oda Nobunaga, after the battle of Okehazama avoided risky, gambling battles.

Ieyasu also fought battels in the safest way. He eventually becomes the Shogun of Japan, but he has said he had three great teachers in his life.

The first was Takeda Shingen, and he taught Ieyasu the way of war.

The second was Nobunaga, and as terrifying as he was, he taught Ieyasu the greatness and the way of being a general.

The third was Hideyoshi, and he taught Ieyasu how to use others.

You can see that he has learned lessons from both friends and foe.

This is a rather hard thing to do. He looked at some of the great men in Japan, and learned from them.

Ieyasu will go on to build the Edo period, but as you can see, the wisdom of other generals are packed in to his regime, which is incredible.

Whether it was for governing or systems, he created it based on the wisdom of many generals such as Hokujo, Takeda, Oda, Toyotomi. Ieyasu indeed was a general with great potential.

The words of Tokugawa Ieyasu
"Burden creates man, a light weight does not"

In training, a larger burden means you get more muscles. Without applying weight on yourself, it does not become a training.

This is the work equivalent of a big project or problem.

If you only do easy work that you are used to, you won't grow.

Dealing with a big project is definitely hard, difficult, and it takes to courage to take on a challenge.

But overcoming it makes us grow.

Both challenging and overcoming challenges makes people what they are.

Unlike the Sengoku period, failure doesn't mean death in

our time so we should face the challenges and increase our skill.

We should be careful when things are going too smoothly.

The harder the problem is, the more we know we can overcome it.

Because an impossible problem never presents itself.

Let's face our difficulties with confidence.

If that benefits us and our society.

＊Try applying Tokugaaw Ieyasu's life to yours

Even Ieyasu, the man who created the Edo bakufu faced many difficulties in life but his dutiful personality brought on a deep trust of others as well.

<Questions>

The amazing thing about Ieyasu is that he learns from his enemies as well, and he has said he learned a lot from Takeda Shingen, who bested him in battle. What have you learned from your failures? Are you making the most of your lessons?

Ieyasu said he learned what it is to be a general, from his ally Nobunaga. This could also be taken as a plan of Ieyasu to become the top. Is rewarding and punishing fair and thorough in your company?

One of Ieyasu's famous words is "Burden makes man". It means power and responsibility makes us grow as a person as well. Are you giving enough burden to the subordinates you want to grow?

Kobayakawa Takakage - foresight is to look into people

Kobayakawa Takakage, the intelligence that supported the Mouri family

Kobayakawa Takakage (1533 ~ 1597)

Born as the third child of Mouri Motonari, he is later

adopted by the Kobayakawa family.

Although the Kobayakawa family was divided when Takakage was adopted, they eventually unified. With his older brothers, Mouri Takamoto and Yoshikawa Motoharu Takakage supported the Mouri family and the three were called the Mouri Ryousen. Talented at battles using the navy, and as one of the first to foresee Hideyoshi's domination, he decided to follow Hideyoshi. Afterwards, with the Mouri family Takakage supports Hideyoshi, and he was treasured as one of his 5 elders. (He was in reality the face of the Mouri family)

In a way, Kobayakawa Takakage was the boss of a subsidiary supporting the unskilled boss of his parent company, Mouri Terumoto.

The foresight of Kobayakawa Takakage

When Nobunaga was betrayed by Akechi Mitsuhide, Takakage was rushing to the aid of Shimizu Muneharu, the lord of Takamatsu castle who was being viciously attacked by Hideyoshi.

Then suddenly, Hideyoshi suggested a peace treaty, the terms being that if Shimizu Muneharu commits seppuku, he would spare all of his soldiers.

Hearing this, Takakage sensed that something had happened.

Since Takakage had been actively collecting information based around Kyoto, he had always paid attention to the situation around him.

Although Nobunaga was at his peak, Takakage had heard from the monk Ankokujiekei who knew both Nobunaga and Hideyoshi well that Nobunaga would soon fall, and that Hideyoshi would probably take his place.

Most other warlords thought nothing of Hideyoshi.

It was commonly thought that if something should happen to Nobunaga, either Ieyasu, his ally or Shibata Katsuie, a trusted elder would take his place, and dominate Japan.

When Takamatsu castle opened up, and Shimizu Muneharu commited seppuku, only then did Takakage learn about Nobunaga's death.

At first Takakage and Yoshikawa Motoharu angered at Hideyoshi realizing that they had been tricked, and the popular vote was to immediately attack Hideyoshi. But just as the pursuit of Hideyoshi seemed to have been decided, Takakage stepped in and said, "We should see how Hideyoshi acts next. If Hideyoshi retreats his army without telling us about Nobunaga's death, that means he had deceived us. However if he should officially notify us of Nobunaga's death, we should accept that as Hideyoshi's quality. Let us wait".

Takakage then proceeded to explain his vision of the future, and explained to others how Hiddeyoshi would probably conquer Japan.

He also talked about how Nobunaga's death should not tempt their desire to conquer Japan.

This is partially due to his respect for Hideyoshi's potential, but it was also because he knew that the young Mouri Terumoto did not have the skill and experience of his father and brothers to accomplish such an achievement. It was a decision made from Takakage's quality to see through people.

Soon a messenger came from Hideyoshi, and the messeager was Kuroda Yoshitaka.

Takakage and Kuroda Yoshitaka would soon become respect each other's skill, but that is a story in the future.

"Lord, Oda Nobunaga has perished at Honnougi, and therefore we will immediately go back to Kyoto".

Even after this message, many claimed that they should attack Hideyoshi.

However, Takakage's heart was set.

Kuroda Yoshitaka continued to say,

"Akechi Mitsuhide was the one who betrayed and murdered our Lord. Therefore we will go back to take our revenge".

Takakage said,

"Understood".

Kuroda Yoshitaka continued,

"It is natural to get revenge for our Lord. However our Lord is already gone. We would like you to join forces with us. We would also like some of your men to come with us".

Many of the elders were angered saying "What ridiculous wishes! Kill him too!" but Takakage said "I understand take as much soldiers as you want".

Hideyoshi actually did go on to fight Akechi Mitsuhide, (the battle of Yamazaki), and it is said that when the Akechi army saw the flags of Mouri within the Hideyoshi army, they lost the will to fight saying "Even Mouri has sided with Hideyoshi".

After that the relationship between Takakage and Hideyoshi becomes stronger, and when Hideyoshi conquered Japan he favored the Mouri family, and assigned Takakage as one his chief staff. Thanks to this, the Mouri family became stable. Hideyoshi never forgot his debt towards Mouri.

Episodes of Kobayakawa Takakage.

It is told that Toyotomi Hideyoshi said "There would be no problem if we leave the governing of the east to Ieyasu, and the governing of the west to Takakage".

That is the level of trust he had earned.

In a conversation with Kuroda Yoshitaka, Takakage said "You are smart and therefore can make decisions instantaneously, but at the same time you probably regret a lot. I am not as smart as you so I consider things with more time so I rarely regret".

When Takakage died Kuroda Yoshitaka mourned deeply, saying that Japan had lost a great wise man.

Before his death, he left 3 wills to Terumoto, his nephew and the heir of the Mouri family. Simply put, the will was

1. Even if the land goes to chaos do not take part in war

2. Do not follow Ankokujiekei's plans

3. Never lend land to nearby countries, for they will ask for it saying they want a port. Then they will try to invade using that as an excuse.

The Mouri family always became what Takakage had predicted it to be.

Takakage used his foresight to protect his family.

His father was a great man, and his brother was intelligent and full of potential.

After their death, Takakage dedicated his life and his talent for his family.

＊Try applying Kobayakawa Takakage's way of life to yourself.

As the third child of the warlord Mouri Motonari, with his father became one of the major forces in Japan ruling over the Chugoku area. However after Motonari's firstborn Takamoto was assassinated Takakage goes on to work for his family in war and diplomacy. He was such a man that even Kuroda Yoshitaka, Hideyoshi's tactician mourned in his death saying that Japan had lost a wise man. Takakage was an intelligent man with a great personality.

<Questions.>

As he was searching a way to compromise with his enemies to save his family, Takakage achieved his family's stability by aiding Hideyoshi, a man who didn't seem powerful at that point. How can you obtain the affection of someone that can make your company greater?

Chapter 3
Work Hacks from the Edo ~ Meiji Era

Uesugi Youzan - the reform that solved a crisis

Uesugi Youzan, the man who overcame a financial crisis.

He will later be called one of the best rulers during the Edo period, but the road he followed was never easy.

Thanks to the works of Uesugi Kenshin, one of the best generals of all time¥, the Uesugi family was always strong even after their defeat due to aiding Ishida Mitsunari and his west army during the age of Kenshin's heir, Kagekatsu. Although their land decreased, the subordinates of Uesugi always found honor in working for the Uesugi family, and refused to leave. However, things went south when their land was reduced to half in the age of the 3rd Shogun, and the economy went into crisis. Even worse, due to heavy taxes the farmers ended up leaving the Yonezawa domain.

Uesugi Kenshin
Jouetsu
1,500,000 goku

Moving to Aizu
1,200,000 goku

To Yonezawa
300,000 goku
Age of Yozan
150,000 goku

* 10,000 goku = 750 million yen

Kokudaka refers to the figure of land productivity shown with koku (goku).

Some farmers couldn't even eat, and a horrible tradition of murdering weak children emerged. The lord before Uesugi Youzan was even considering giving back the land to the Shogunate, and so Youzan became the feudal lord in an incredibly harsh time.

This is where his reform starts.

What he did first was,

Give offering to the shrine

· to remind parents of their duty

· to not neglect education and martial arts

· to not forget frugality

· to reward and punish properly

He vowed to do these things through worshipping at the shrine.

To start transformation meant to change not just the officials but to involve the people who lived in the domain as well. And to accomplish this he created a system to hear their voices.

And this lead to the creation of the
Jousho-bako

Although not anonymously, anyone, even if they were farmers, could send an opinion if they wrote down their name and address.

Also, since the goal was to increase the people's wealth, rather than just focusing on frugality, there was a need to create a new industry. So, with the order of frugality, the growth of industries and education of farmers were encouraged.

The great order of frugality

Only a one-plate meal was permitted for daily food, clothes were limited to those made from cotton, silk was prohibited, the number of maidens were decreased to 9 from the original 50. Even more, they checked the account books in detail, and thoroughly looked for luxuries. Because the lords were living simple lives, slowly the common people of the land started to live simply as well.

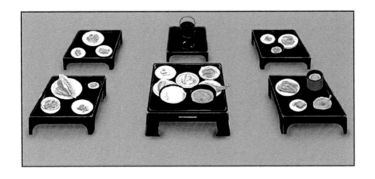

Ichiju Issai

They were trying to limit expense. What did they next was,

Growth of Industry.

The Yonezawa domain had no local industry. So the growth of this became the main focusing point.
They decided to create a textile industry in the land, using ramie as the main ingredient, they developed silk from

silkworms. Even more, they put strength in industries as pottery and Japanese paper (washi).

Since they need a merchant to sell the products they made, choosing products that could compete in the Kyoto market, asked the merchants for cooperation and slowly but surely increased their income.

Encouraging Farming

Agriculture was also developing, and even the lord himself went out to plow the land, which was something that never happened.

Samurai's never farmed, but with the economic crisis even the samurai's were sent out to farm and they gave all their strength to creating new farms, maintaining roads and repairing facilities.

To prepare for starvation, they advertised hedge and tea, and requested families to plant fruits with seed such as persimmon, and to keep carp for food.

The "Katemono" was also maid. This was something Youzan ordered the local doctors to make, which was booklet about food other than rice or wheat, how to eat them and how to store them. This was handed out to all the families throughout the land. On the booklet was 82 different alternative food that could be used for a main meal, and this was a great help when starvation did come. In fact, this eventually went on to become the local cuisine of the area.

The spirit of the reform was,

- Cut anything unnecessary and create new jobs
- Everyone must be on the same page
- Each family will set a goal to achieve
- If the goal is not achieved they must change their ways
- Punish and reward accordingly. Even a man in power must be punished if necessary.
- Give opinions often, and treasure good opinion wherever

it came from

· Quit unnecessary customs

The fire movement

This was the movement to "Burn coal with the fire in your heart, and give the fire to your neighbors".

When Youzan first came to Yonezawa it was a cold winter.

On his way he made a campfire and spent the night, but the fire went out to ashes quickly.

Like this country, are there only ashes? he thought.

As he was pondering, he poked the weakening fire, and found a small fire on a coal.

The fire was not dead yet. Youzan blew on the small fire, and started up the fire again.

Youzan was inspired by this, saying "I want all of you to be this coal. I will be too", and continued, "Each one of us has coal in their hearts, and some are lit but some are not. If you already have fire, I want you to share it with others. That way, this cold Yonezawa domain will be warm again. I'll be the source of fire as well, so I want all of you to be as well".

Everyone in the Yonezawa domain started to work together.

If you put your mind to it, you can do mostly everything.

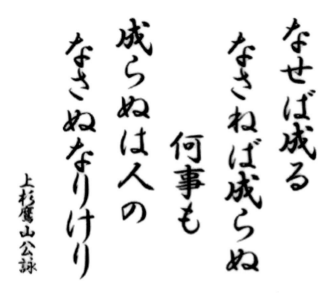

なせば成る
なさねば成らぬ
何事も
成らぬは人の
なさぬなりけり
上杉鷹山公詠

(Do and it will be done

Don't and it won't be done.

Everything that isn't done is due to not doing anything.)

These are famous words. Originally the words of Takeda Shingen, "Do and it will be done, don't and it won't be done, oh the frailty of those who whine it can't be done", Youzan said those words based on this.

From frugality to developing new industries, the reforms

93

made success to the point that the domain was able to have savings. And even more when the great starvation hit the country the Yonezawa domain did not lose as much people as other domains.

Youzan's was reformed was based on the reforms by Naoe Kanetsugu.

When the Uesugi family lost land in Aizu, Kanetsugu, the elder at the time orchestrated a similar reform creating industries and worked hard for his people. Kanetsugu had been considered useless until them, but after Youzan visited his grave over 200 times, his reputation was recoverd.

Denkoku no Ji

The state is inherited from one's ancestors and passed on to one's descendants; it should not be administered selfishly.

The people belong to the state; they should not be administered selfishly.

The lord exists for the sake of the state and the people: the state and the people do not exist for the sake of the lord.

Never forget these 3 articles.

This is what Youzan told his successor.

Youzan's achievements will go on to be known overseas, thanks to one book.

Uchimura Kanzo and his book, "Representative Men of Japan", was read throughout the western world.

Other than Uesugi Youzan, people such as Saigo Takamori, Ninomiya Sontoku, Nakae Toju, Nichiren were introduced in the book.

Uesugi Youzn became famous in recent years due to JFK's speech.

Kennedy has said that Uesugi Youzan was the Japanese he respected the most.

Ambassador Kennedy also has spoken about how her father respected Youzan.

Although the story of Uesugi Youzan is one from the past, it is all true, and it speaks to us even now.

Uesugi Youzan is considered the best out of the best of the lords, and it was probably due to his humbleness that he succeeded.

Someone with power must have a quality.

I have talked about Youzan feeling this.

＊Try applying Youzan's life to yours.

Youzan is considered one the best lords of the Edo period, having saved his domain from a hopeless crisis. He was an intelligent and noble man, which even JFK has expressed his respect.

<Questions>

In reforming the helpless Yonezawa domain, Uesugi Youzan first went to worship at a shrine. He went to admonish himself, to save his people. Have you shown your dedication to work for society?

To reform his domain Youzan placed a system to hear the voices of his people. However, this also had the goal to find useful individuals. Have you researched your surroundings? Are you working on finding better talent?

Sending out an order of frugality Uesugi Youzan himself lived on a simple diet, changed his clothes to something cheaper and made himself an example. Are you an example?

In preparation for starvation, a booklet was handed out about eating different diets. Are you prepared for worst case scenarios?

Sakamoto Ryoma   outstanding knowledge and
action that drove the Meiji Restoration

Sakamoto Ryoma promoter of the Meiji Restoration,
accomplished the Satcho alliance, Taisei Hokan and
Kaientai.

One of the most popular historical figures in Japan, his

foresight was incredible. He was a rare man who could see from a wide perspective called "Japan".

Sakammoto Ryoma (1836 ~ 1867)

He was the mentor of the Meiji Restoration, and was born in a wealthy merchant family.

In his young days, he was bullied and weak known as the "bed wetter". However, his sister Otome educated him and taught him martial arts, and in swordsmanship he became so strong that he had no competition in Tosa. And because of this, he goes to Edo to pursuit swordsmanship.

There he met Katsura Kogoro (Kido Takayoshi), his master
Katsu Kaishu, and increased his sword skills. Going to Edo
had a great impact on his life.

In his youth, he visited the merchant family of Kawashima
with his sister often, and he saw various foreign goods. His
interest in overseas must have been grown here.

Utilizing his foresight, he started many projects for the

future of Japan.

He left the world at the young age of 32, but he was an essential existence in the Meiji Restoration.

He started 3 big projects within a span of 5 and a half years.

It is incredible how someone young, and someone who used to be a coward saw the vision of Japan in the future, and set out to accomplish it.

Even the opposing forces of Satsuma and Choshu did not have a clear vision on what to do after they had defeated the Shogunate. There is a famous story about how after the Shogunate was thrown and a new government took its place, the top of Satsuma, Shiamadu Hissamitsu thought he was going be the new Shogun.

Both Satsuma and Choshu were astounded by Sakamoto Ryoma's clear vision the future.

Sakamoto Ryoma's big projects
1. Assembling the opposing forces against the Shogunate. The alliance between Satsuma and Choshu

2. Drafting the new government

3. Creation of the Tosa Kaientai. Japan's first stock fueled organization and also at the same time a political association.

*his work for the Taise Hokan is a big project, but we included it within number 2

Looking at it one by one, he first coordinated the Sacho alliance. Satsuma and Choshu had been enemies for a long time, but Sakamoto Ryoma's success was accomplished because Ryoma was close to the leaders of both domains, Katsura Kogoro of Choshu and Saigou Takamori of Satsuma.

Both Satsuma and Choshu knew the importance of teaming up for the new government, but had difficulty becoming partners. This is where Sakamoto Ryoma came in, and the alliance was made.

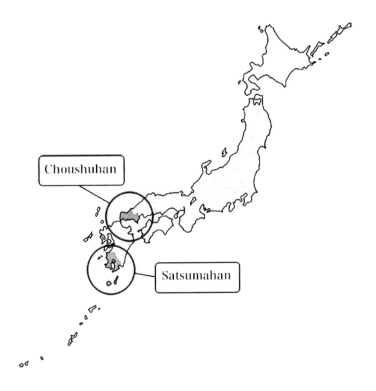

With the alliance, the two Shogunate opposing forces got together, and soon Tosa, Geishu and Higo joined, and became a force great enough to fight the Shougunate. Next was the draft of the government called the "Senchuhassaku" Sakamoto Ryoma knew that the foreign countries will become part of the civil war. He envisioned a modern unified stated under the Japanese emperor.

He planned for many things, such as the restoration of the government, construction of a parliament, treaties with foreign states, establishment of a constitution and a creation of a national army. He even wrote down concrete individuals who would be perfect for each positon. Sakamoto Ryoma wanted a restoration without a civil war, but this felt futile for the Satsuma and Choshu, who were trying to defeat the Shogunate with force. Most historians think this was the cause of his assassination.

Ryoma unfortunately died before the restoration was completed, but the Senchuhassaku became the basis of the new government.

Even more, both a parliament and a constitution were created in the middle of the Meiji period.

Ryoma's foresight might have been to the point that it was seeing too far.

What makes Ryoma incredible, is that he had the ability to create and plan for the things he saw.

The venture called the Tosa Kaientai

The Kaientai that Sakamoto Ryoma created was more than just a trading company, also being a government association and even a navy.

And the creation of this association is where we truly see Ryoma's foresight and insight.

Taking a few lines from the principle of the Kaientai,

1. Only those who left the Shogunate, or have gone overseas
may join this association
2. We make profit while having incentive, developing and
speculating the country, and supporting our domain (Tosa)

When he said having incentive, he may have also meant to

try anything that could bring profit. Overall they created industries of trade, shipping, finance and construction. He was probably trying to create a conglomerate after the Meiji restoration had ended.

In reality, after the death of Ryouma Iwazaki Shotaro became his successor, and inherited his ideas and went on to create the massive Mitsubishi conglomerate.

Ryoma was not man of strange ideas, but a man of foresight and insight. And from this perspective, we can see the reasons behind his actions.

From his life, we can learn how important connections and information is.

His master, Katsu Kaishu was at the center of the Shogunate, and other than important men like Saigo Takamori and Katsura Kogoro, he also had connections with the foreign merchant Grabber. Thanks to the friendship with these people, Ryoma was able to obtain a wide perspective and a vast amount of information, and went on to form his ideas. You cannot deny Ryoma's flexibility as well. There is a possibility that there were others with Ryoma's foresight. But we know Ryoma because he acted and accomplished something, and that is what sets him apart from others.

This was Japan's popular hero, Sakamoto Ryoma.

＊Try applying Sakamoto Ryoma's life to yours.

Popular in Japan, Ryoma was essential in making Japan what it is now.

\<Questions\>

The two forces that Sakamoto Ryoma mediated, Satsuma and Choshu were both forces opposing the Shogunate, but with the conflict between them their alliance was difficult to accomplish. However Ryoma persuaded both of them to set their differences aside for a better Japan. As a company should you set out to work for society?

In the middle of taking down the Shogunate, while others focused on defeating the enemy Ryoma was able to see the future. That was probably because his saw defeating the Shogunate not as the goal, but as part of the process to create a new Japan. Do you have a clear vision and/or plan for your life?

Saigo Takamori Work with the heavens, not people

The hero of the Meiji restoration.

Saigo Takamori is described both as a politician and a soldier, but in reality he is much more than that, to the point it's difficult to accurately describe him.

Katsu Kaishu calls Saigo Takamori "高士(koshi)", meaning

an outstanding character.

With so many qualities being a politician, soldier and even an educator, you see a different side to him every time you change your perspective.

So for this time, we'll look at the way he works by taking a look at a slice of him, as a soldier and a politician.

Originally, Saigo was a clerk but Shimazu Nariakira noticed his potential, and Saigo went on to be one of the most important figures in Japanese history. The question is, however, why was he discovered in the first place?

This is due to Shimazu Nariakiar's way of discovering useful individuals by openly listening to the voices of his subordinates.

One day Saigo gives his opininon to Shimazu Nariakira. Although what he said is not written down, it had something to do with farming and governing. This led to him being noticed by Shimazu, and Saigo learned under him by working as his personal assistance. This had an enormous effect on Saigo.

The meetings with many powerful and ambitious people and Shimazu stimulated Saigo. And on top of that, his thirst of knowledge led to creating a foundation of a man who would accomplish something that will be remembered in history.

Saying opinions to your elders

If Saigo had not spoken up to Shimazu Nariakira, he would never have been promoted and maybe the Meiji restoration wouldn't have happened either. However speaking up requires a lot of courage.

Perhaps the first necessary step is courage.

Actively seeking new connections.

Even in the chaos that was the end of the Edo period, Saigo went around talking to experts and intelligent people for information, and to understand the situation.

It is also said that Saigo was very polite, even if the person he was talking to was very young.

Thanks to these attributes, Saigo became very popular, and there were a numerous amounts of request to have a meeting with him

In the midst of his master and godlike figure Shimadu Naoakira's sudden death, and his ever changing surroundings, Saigo prepared for death many times.

Self-sacrifice is necessary sometimes.

In his later years, Saigo says "Only someone who doesn't need fame or life can change the country in the face of great difficulty". This probably came from Saigo's own experience.

While coming up with realistic solutions he also gave everything he had, even his life, to solve a difficult problem. And it is said that his decisions were always accurate.

When the Meiji restoration was completed, and the new government started, the authoritative figures of the government went on the Iwakura mission to see foreign countries.

Meanwhile Saigo stayed behind to govern Japan. It is said that during the time Saigo was in power, the discontent of the people dropped drastically.

"Politics is to serve the heavens, that is integral, and it must be done by someone who does not need power or fame. " Saying this, Saigo lived a simple life in a simple house, wearing simple clothes. Thanks to this, many people accepted and understood him.

If Saigo had seized the chance of the Meiji restoration, and had gained power to live a luxurious life, there may have been a movement similar to the restoration again.

One example of this is the decisive action of the Satsuma.

Okubo, and Kido, both at the center of the new government were still in fierce debate about when to change Satsuma into a prefecture.

Saigo opens his mouth, saying

"If both of you are considering small procedures, we must forcefully act. If they raise an army and war happens, I will take the responsibility and face them so be reassured. "

Okubo and Kido both were glad at Saigo's proposition, and decided to forcefully set Satsuma as a prefecture.

And although the rise of armies were expected, this didn't happen (thanks to Saigo's preparation of keeping the main armies of the Meiji restoration of Choshu and Satsuma together, and aiming state of the art cannons toward each area). Even the Haihanchiken, considered to be the biggest rebellion in Meiji restoration, was solved peacefully thanks to Saigo's work.

Giving everything and planning

These were the characteristics of Saigo's work.

Later years, he loses his life in the Seinan war, but this could be taken as him sensing the end of his duty, after accomplishing such a thing as the Meiji restoration. It is also speculated that if Saigo had really taken command in that war, he wouldn't have fought the way it was fought.

Interestingly, there are no photos of Saigo himself. The Saigo we picture is actually an image formed through the description of his relatives. We'd like to sow you some photos thought to be Saigo in recent years.

The one on the right is thought to be Saigo. On his left is Komatsu Kiyokado, and in the center is Okubo Toshimitsu.

Let's look at it closer.

This is the photo thought to be the most closest to his real face.

He seems to have intensity, with a hint of kindness.

We'll end this chapter by introducing Saigo's words.

Respect the heavens and love humanity.
This was Saigo Takamori, the greatest out of the greatest.

＊Try applying Saigo Takamori's life to yours.
One of the essential figures of the Meiji Restoration and a successful army general、 he suicides at the end of the conflict with the new government.

<Questions>

From when Saigo Takamori was a low class samurai, he actively expressed his opinions. This required courage, even more so considering the time. However, thanks to this he was picked up by Shimazu Naoakira and rose to power. Is there someone you want to bring up the courage to express your opinion towards?

Even in the chaos that is the end of an era, Saigo Takamori never ceased to interact with people. One of the reason to do this was to gain enough information to understand the world. Are you interacting with enough people?

On the subject of facing difficulties, Saigo Takamori has said "Do not work for people, but the heavens". When making a decision, Saigo has considered if that goes with heavens. What does it mean to decide with the heavens?

Okubo Toshimichi　Letting Subordinates Work to their Fullest

Ookubo Toshimichi, the elder of the Meiji restoration.

Okubo Toshimichi (1830 ~ 1878)
One of the big three of the Meiji restoration, alongside Saigo Takamori and Kido Takayoshi.

Born in Satsuma, he originally was just a low class samurai.

He grew up with his old friend and companion Saigo Takamori, originally meeting him in school. He was never good at martial arts, but he was talented in reading.

When his father was fired from his job, the Okubo family experienced sever poverty.

There were times when he would to Saigo's house to eat food, but when the meal ended it was said he would quietly put things away, bow, and leave.

How to be noticed by a key person

When Okubo Toshimichi learned that the substantial leader of Satsuma (Shimazu Hisamitsu) enjoyed playing go and often played against the priests who were living at the shrine, he sent out numerous letters writing about his view on the government.

He continued this for over 3 years.

Eventually he was granted a meeting with Shimazu Hisamitsu, was picked for the position of treasurer, became part of politics, and even went on to have great influence by becoming a close associate of Hisamitsu.

After that with Satsuma as his shield, he becomes the driving force of the Meiji restoration alongside Saigo Takammori.

Work hacks of Okubo Toshimichi

Although Saigo Takamori and Kido Takayoshi were both incredibly intelligent, after the Meiji restoration was accomplished there was a great need for a completely new government organization and for a new head.

It was critical for the new government to stabilize the chaos within the country in order to rush modernization.

And this is where Okubo Toshimichi's skill was needed.

The original Meiji government is considered to be a government created by Satsuma, but Okubo talked about his people from Satsuma as "Useful in war, but not in politics". He ignored favoring his heritage and told the people from other areas "You guys work for Japan, not Satsuma and Choshu. Have honor in the fact that you work for the country", and treated everyone equally.

However, because of this while he was popular amongst the people outside of Satsuma and Choshu, he wasn't as popular in Satsuma, his home.

After the restoration had been completed he constructed the Ministry of Home Affairs, and appointed himself on top. And although there were other Ministries, he became the substantial supreme authority in Japan. The Ministry of Home Affairs was a giant ministry, including agriculture, international relationships, education, health, and the police.

Since the next step was the modernization of Japan, it was critical to start several projects with speed in order to make Japan a powerful country.

Due to this it is said that Okubo Toshimichi valued skill over heritage, brought in numbers of intelligent individuals and assigned them to various posts.

The men who gathered together selflessly for Japan, goes on to create the foundation of Modern Japan in an incredibly short amount of time. It is said that some of the systems constructed them have been inherited by present Japan. To create such a solid system in such an amount time is something truly astounding.

Okubo's way of working in the new government was always the same.

It is a workstyle found in his home, Satsuma as well.

The way was to choose subordinates carefully,

And to ignore explaining details and only giving the main goal and purpose, saying

"Give it everything you got, and I'll take all the responsibility".

People from all over the country had gathered to put Japan on their shoulders and to give themselves up for a new Japan. And although it must have been impossible to micro manage everything due to the amount of work there was, the people who have worked for Okubo later said, "I gave everything I had to my work, it was hard but I was able to work without worry".

One of these men is Maejima Hisoka.

Maejima Hisoka, born in Etigo and created Japan's postal system.

Famous for creating Japan's postal system, Maeshima was one of the people who showed his skill under Okubo. Not only did he work on the postal system, but he drafted the "Sanshinhou",

The Sanshihou is consisted form three factors, all with the aim to connect the central agency to each area of Japan. Maejima had shown his skill in creating systems as well.

This is something that lives on right now.

Originally the top of Fukui, Sasaki had been sent to Australia to research the silk industry.

When Sasaki returned, he was summoned by Okubo, and was appointed the task of creating the entire silk industry.

When Sasaki advised that they should first create a spinning factory in Japan, Okubo said, "Get on it immediately".

And this was how the first spinning mill of Japan was created in Gunma.

Even more, Okubo thought it was essential to repair and improve Japan's port for modernization.

When he learned that the Netherlands were skilled in this area, he immediately appointed a young Dutch man who wasn't even 30 to be in charge of all the construction of ports and canals in Japan.

The monthly pay was a mind blowing 300 yen a month (modern equivalent of 5 million yen). The name of the Dutch man was Johannis de Rijke.

Although he was Dutch, he left his name in the history of Japan.

He stayed in Japan for over 30 years, and successfully accomplished the task given by Okubo.

Okubo was also trying to modernize agriculture. When he heard that Maeda Masana had bought high quality seedlings from Paris, Okubo immediately ordered him to grow the seeds in Satsuma. Maeda was amazed at the fact Okubo had the time to think about seeds, since they were in the middle of the Seinan war.

Ignoring personal emotions and being fair

Bold ways of giving tasks.

These attitudes became the driving force of creating a modern Japan, and has become the foundation of what Japan is now.

Okubo's workstyle is something that can be found in Satsuma as well.

Basically, entrusting an outstanding subordinate to do the job.

Only explaining the purpose and importance of the

job.

The way of, "Give it all you got!"

It's an incredible way to do a job.

Even though Okubo wasn't as popular as Saigo in his hometown, he is definitively a figure we can learn a lot from.

Man of integrity, Okubo Toshimichi

He was very pure when it came to money. It was also found out that the new and weak government had no funds, and it was later revealed that time to time Okubo would put in his own money to fund the government.

After the death of Okubo, it was found that although he only had 140 yen as assets, he held a debt of over 8000 yen (more than 200 million yen today). Although all of his income was in mortgage, no one came demanding for repayment, understanding Okubo's motives. As for the debt, a part of it was paid by the government, and a part of it was paid from donations. Being a person who literally gave everything he had for his projects, he was more of a statesman than a politician, alongside people like Oda Nobunaga, Toyotomi Hideyasu and Tokugawa Ieyasu.

In a sense, it is ironic how Okubo, who took down the Shogunate, has said he learned from Tokugawa Ieyasu the most, the man who built the Shogunate.

*Try applying Ookubo Toshimichi's life to yours
After the completion of the Meiji restoration, he became the key figure in building the foundation of Japan.

<Question>

Okubo to prove himself, spent a long time to create a connection with a key person. It was a result of Okobo's willpower and tenacity. Have you tried forming a connection with a key person?

The new government held numerous amounts of jobs, and it was impossible to do it all by himself. So Okubo told his young employees only the purpose and importance of each job, and let them finish each task the way they wanted to. By this way, Okubo succeeded in educating his men as speeding up the jobs. Should you try trusting your employees to educate them?

Takasugi Shinsaku The Militia that Completely Changed Tactics

Takasugi Shinsaku Created one of the first armies of the Meiji Restoration

Without the actions of this amazing man, the Meiji Restoration might have taken up more time.

He was brave, his tactics were on the point, and as soon as he changed the course of history, he died.

Sakamoto Ryoma also leaves this world early, but Takasui Shinsaku lived as if his only purpose was starting the drive of the Meiji Restoration.

He died at the age of 27, but he learned at the famous Matsushitamura School, where famous people who would be key figures in the Restoration also studied, such as Itou Hirobumi and Yamagata Alitomo. Alongside Kusaka Genzui was considered the genius of the generation.

A lot of the students at the Matsushitamura School came from a lower status family, but Takasugi Shinsaku was born in a high class family, and perhaps because of that his parents didn't approve him going to the school. He will eventually marry such a beautiful woman others thought Takasugi Shinsaku would drop all his ambitions, but even she was not enough to stop the energy of Takasugi Shinsaku. Shinsaku first learned at a local school, then went on to learn at Matsushitamura, then to a school at Edo. When he learned that Yoshida Shoin, his teacher had been put to jail he went to visit him many times. Yoshida Shoin was executed while Shinsaku was on his way back to Choshu from Edo.

Yoshida Shoin was known for his thorough behaviorism,

leaving such words as "What is learning without action".
His actions must have had a great impact on his students,
including Shinsaku.

Going to Shanghai

After coming back from Edo, he found interest in the navy.
A part of this was due to Japan's ideology at the time of
regarding all foreigners as enemies and destroying them,
which inevitably led to the emphasis on the navy. (you can
also say he learned this from Yoshida Shoin as well)

He decided to ride a ship to Edo, and through his journey
and schooling met with important figures such as Sakuma
Shozan, and Yokoi Shonan. And to widen his perspective, he
went as far as Tohoku

After that, he goes to Qing (China) as an attendant of the
Shogunate from Nagasaki, alongside Godai Tomoatu, who
was also from Satsuma. However Qing had already started
to become a colony of the western world, and as he learned
the history of how this had happened, he must have realized
that "If Japan doesn't chase now, we would also become a
colony. We must change the way things are."

The education at Shanghai became very important for
Shinsaku.

Right after his return to Japan, the Barley Incident
happened. This was the incident were a British man tried

to cross on horseback right in front of the lord of Satsuma without bowing, and since he didn't change his behavior after several warnings, the enraged samurai cut him down. This will eventually lead to the war between Satsuma and the British.

After hearing this Shinsaku decided Choshu must act to aid Satsuma, but despite all of his plans none seemed to work.

The only plan that did work was burning away the British Embassy which was in construction, but it also resulted in Shinsaku being sent back to Choshu.

Building a militia

When Choshu attacked a foreign ship using cannons from the Kanmon Channel, they were devastated by the bombing from the British and French. During this battle Shinsaku was in charge of guarding the Shimonoseki. However they only had a few soldiers. They had no weapons. So Shinsaku built a militia, recruiting volunteering soldiers ignoring all social status, different from the main army of Choshu. This militia could be observed as the collapse of the status system that lasted throughout the Edo period.

This was the first time that men who weren't samurai's fought in the army.

During this time at Kyoto Satsuma and Aizu had just formed an alliance, and the battle between Choshu and Satsuma/Aizu had started. Because of this, Choshu lost the war, Shinsaku Lost his friend Kusaka Genzui, and Choshu became the enemy of the state.

Even more the union fleet of Britain, France, American and the Netherlands had invaded Shimonoseki. It was a complete defeat.

The militia would go on to be used during the Meiji restoration as well, and it was a powerful army.

This was due to a strategical factor, made possible by changing weapons in to western ones.

Until then, the main way for Japan to fight was for a dense army to be commanded by a commander. However, being gathered in one place meant it was easier for the enemy to focus fire. So for the militia, Shinsaku decided to disperse his soldiers so that they could each fight on their own decisions.

He taught each soldier the strategy so that they wouldn't need a commander.

To make the soldiers mobile, they didn't wear armor.

Even more, due to the nature of running around in a fight, training included running 50 kilometers in 8 hours, martial arts and sumo wrestling. Training also included education. Shinsaku taught his soldiers philosophers such as Mencius, promoted those who were intelligent, and discharged those who couldn't train properly.

His innovation in the army somewhat reminds us of Nobunaga.

Win in negotiations even if you lost the war

Choshu appointed Shinsaku for their diplomatic negotiations. They chose him for his high status and courage. Takasugi Shinsaku is probably the first to negotiate after a defeat against four countries.

The four countries demanded a lot in this negotiation, but Shinsaku agreed to most of them. Japan's military is no match against foreigners. If so, we should encourage the trade between Japan and other countries, so that Japan could gain power. This was Shinsaku's reasoning.

One of the main debates during the negotiation was about leasing the land to foreign countries, but Shinsaku did not yield this.

If he accepted it, Japan would become a colony like Shanghai. When the four countries shouted, "Why won't you concede!? You lost!" In response, Shinsaku simply read aloud from the "Kojiki", explaining patiently what kind of country Japan was. Shinsaku succeeded in withdraw their demand of leasing the land. It is said that Shinsaku read from the "Kojiki" to explain Japan was a country of the Emperor, but the truth is unknown.

Choshu at this time was in a horrible state, being deemed enemy of the state and being invaded by other nations. It was on the verge of extinction.

The popular vote was for Choshu to be controlled by the Shogunate, and the Shogunate did come to demand the dissolution of Choshu's army.

Shinsaku's militia was very popular due to its nature for ignoring social status and negating the feudal system.

The Shogunate raised an army to take over Choshu, and with conservatives gaining power in Choshu, Shinsaku and his followers were running out of options.

The Kouzanji Rally

If the militia and army should be disbanded, there would be

no means to defeat the conservatives and the Shogunate, therefore there can be no Meiji Restoration.

If the Restoration does not get achieved, Choshu will collapse.

The first step is to fight the conservatives at the top of Choshu. After that the Shogunate.

Shinsaku went around the soldiers saying, this is the time to rise.

At first only 70 soldiers gathered.

Utilizing surprise attacks, they will eventually gain control over Choshu, but there was actually a powerful supporter for them.

The merchants and townspeople inspired by Shinsaku

With the economy going south at the time, both the merchants and townspeople were having a tough life. Since nothing seemed to be changing for the better, they put their hope in Shinsaku, who was trying to create a new era without social status and a feudal state. They supported Shinsaku with money and goods, and this aid will soon come from all over Choshu.

They gave everything they had for Shinsaku's movement.

Even though the small army only had 70 people at the start, with each win the word spread, and the number of soldiers slowly increased. In the end they got control of Choshu, and started to focus on defeating the Shogunate.

Statue of Takasugi Shinsaku

The army Shinsaku led got new leaders, so Shinsaku became in charge of the navy.

And with that, Shinsaku starts to import state of the art weapons. Right before this, thanks to Sakamoto Ryoma the alliance between Satsuma and Choshu had been formed. Due to this Satsuma did not join the second invasion against Choshu, and after that Satsuma also starts to fight the Shogunate.

Against the Shogunate's Ogura castle, Shinsaku struggled to conquer it, since the Shogunate forces were giving their full strength with their power on the line. In the end however, Shinsaku conquered Ogura castle, and with Omura Masujiro, utilizing new weapons defeating the Shogunate all over the place, the Shogunate finally had to retreat.

However, Shinsaku dies in the middle of the battle aginst Ogura castle, due to tuberculosis.

The defeat of the Tokugawa Shogunate would be soon, but Shinsaku unfortunately passed away before the sunrise of the Meiji Restoration happened.

Although Shinsaku was a man that accomplished so much in his life, he like jokes, drinking, and he was popular amongst the ladies.

Shinsuke had given Ryoma a pistol he brought from Shanghai. When Ryoma saw Shinsuke playing the Shamisen as he commanded the war against Ogura castle, he thought "I've never seen a man with such a steady nerve. We'll win this war. The enemy doesn't have a commander like this".

Takasugi Shinsaku first learned at a local school, then under Yoshida Shoin who bloomed his intelligence, connected with influential figures at Edo, saw the face of foreign countries at Shanghai, and maybe saw his life's purpose.

Even now, reading, interacting with top class people, and seeing the actual site is the best and most effective way to learn. For Shinsaku, it was clear that he had to study to act. So it must have been clear to him what was important and what was not.

Many people appear in the turn of an era. Takasugi Shinsaku is one of the essential figures of this time, and we can learn a lot from his short life.

＊Try applying Taksuigi Shinsaku's life to yours.

Famous for creating the militia, with his ingenious military commanding he was the pioneer in defeating the Shogunate.

<Questions>

Against the regular army of Choshu, Shinsaku's army was second in line. However due to Shinsaku's way of employing people despite their social status, we can observe the collapse of the social status system here. Is there a way for you to utilize figures from other than your direct subordinates?

Using new western weapons, militia changed the way they fought as well. The mainstream way of fighting in Japan was to fight as a group, but with the change in weapons Shinsuke fought by dispersing his soldiers, rather than gathering them. With this new tactic, he managed to defeat a great army. What is the state of the art technology we should be utilizing?

Pushed into a corner, Shinsaku starts an army at Kouzanji, but it was an act that required him to risk his life He risked his life for his dream and will. Even at a disadvantage, he goes on to defeat his enemies. Do you have a will? Can you explain it in one word?

Afterword

The passage in this book are all originally from my blog, and I assembled this so that I could one day look back on it.

Looking back, I started to read books thanks to the comic book on Oda Nobunaga.

The fact that Nobunaga, who was called a retard in his early years went on to be such a great man gave me a sense of strange confidence. As a member of society and as people who live in a rapidly changing world, I think there are still things we can learn from history.

I express my gratitude towards my staff who helped me go through with it, and my wife Atsuko who takes care of me and my family.

2019/07

Hironobu Ishikawa

Useful for Business
The Work Hacks of Great Japanese Men
What would you do ?

Author   Hironobu Ishikawa

Publisher   G/REX JapaN Co., Ltd.

Editor   Omoikanebooks

Issue Date   18/04/2020

Publishing house

G/REX Japan Co.,Ltd.

Homareya Bld.3F, 2437-2, Goi, Ichihara-shi, Chiba,

290-0056, Japan   +81 436-63-3015

http://www.g-rexjapan.co.jp

•Blog

http://www.g-rexjapan.co.jp/ishikawahironobu/

•facebook

https://www.facebook.com/profile.php?id=100008576345175

•twitter

https://twitter.com/grexhiro

ISBN 978-4-907411-26-8   C0020